WINDOWS OF WORSHIP

trust

trust

WINDOWS OF WORSHIP™

When I'm
FACING TOUGH TIMES

:: DEVOTIONAL JOURNAL ::

Greg Allen ▪ Rick Rusaw ▪ Dan Stuecher
Paul S. Williams, *Editor*

Standard
PUBLISHING

© 2004 CNI Holdings Corp., Windows of Worship is a Trademark of
Christian Network, Inc.

Published by Standard Publishing, Cincinnati, Ohio. A division of Standex
International Corporation. Printed in China.

Cover and interior design by Rule29.

Discover where to watch *Worship* in your town by logging on to
www.Worship.net.

ISBN 0-7847-1515-7

09 08 07 06 05 04   9 8 7 6 5 4 3 2 1

We were made to worship...

The first song I remember Grandma Stone singing to me was "Jesus Loves Me." As a three-year-old I sat on her lap on the front porch swing and asked her to sing it over and over again. Before my daughter Jana could speak, she hummed the same tune, its melody unmistakable as she played on the family room floor. We were made to worship.

To worship God is to walk through the shadows into a familiar welcoming place, where the fire never dies and the light is soft and glowing. To worship God is to know we are truly home, acting on a desire deep in our souls. Long before we rationally understand the truth of Christ, we want to praise someone or something for bringing love and beauty, joy and hope into the world.

At the Christian Network, our desire is simple. Whether through the written page or the television screen, we hope these words and images will draw you to worship, as we thank our Creator for breathing life and love into his creation.

PAUL S. WILLIAMS
Chairman of the Board of Stewards
The Christian Network, Inc.

An Answer to Pain

In this world you will have trouble. But take heart! I have overcome the world.

AN ANSWER TO PAIN

I hate to admit it, but I go through long stretches where life just looks pretty gray. My mind often asks: *What does God think of all the suffering and pain in the world?*

I'd like to say I have always endured suffering without complaint, but I'd be lying. For the better part of three years I was plagued by physical pain that came when it wanted and refused to leave no matter what. I said "Why me?" a lot. But nowhere in the entire Bible will you find the answer to the "Why me?" question. The book of Job is a story about suffering. All the way through, you're convinced that when you get to the end, God's finally going to explain suffering once and for all. But he doesn't. When Job gets angry and challenges God about his suffering, God doesn't so much answer as condescend. "Where were you when I laid the earth's foundations?" "Have you ever given orders to the morning, or shown the dawn its place?" "Does the hawk take flight by your wisdom?" (Job 38:4, 12; 39:26).

Basically, in answer to the question "Why me, Lord?" God says to Job—"I'm God, and you're not."

The Bible never does seem to answer the question, "Why must I suffer?" The subject comes up often enough, but there's never much of a direct answer. Finally I realized pain is a question that seldom finds an answer on this side of eternity. That's what God was saying when he said to Job—"I'm God, and you're not." I may not like God's answer, but it's the only one I'm going to get. It's not for me to know why suffering exists. Instead, God wants me to ask a different question: *How should I respond to pain and suffering?*

It's easy to see God's response to pain and suffering. He sent his Son to Earth to suffer and die. He then invites me to trust his Son with my pain and suffering; to trust the one who found life on the other side of death; to trust Him to serve as my companion and guide on the same frightening journey.

Then the question moves from "Why me?" to "Will I trust the one who journeys with me?" And that's not a question for God to answer. That's a question I must answer. How I answer that question is the most important decision I will ever make.

—*Paul S. Williams*

7

What circumstances in your life have caused you to ask "Why me?" Did you ever receive an answer to that question?

How does knowing that Jesus entered into suffering help you trust him in the midst of yours?

_____

_____

_____

_____

_____

_____

_____

_____

_____

_____

_____

_____

A Hole in One

Just as the sufferings of Christ flow over into our lives, so also through Christ our comfort overflows. If we are distressed, it is for your comfort and salvation; if we are comforted, it is for your comfort, which produces in you patient endurance.

2 corinthians 1:5, 6

A HOLE IN ONE

Bill Hayes was born in America, but grew up attending school on a military base in England. There were many rules there, and Bill didn't do very well with rules. At least that's what the school said when they kicked him out. It was the second time he'd been kicked out of school. Frustrated, Bill's father made his delinquent son get a job at a golf course. He wasn't sure why, but somehow he thought it would be good for him.

It was there that Bill swung a golf club for the first time and something magical happened. From that moment on, the troubled teen knew what he wanted—to be the greatest golfer in the world.

There is something redemptive about golf. Maybe it's the discipline and the mental toughness of the game. Or maybe it's that a person is forced to face his own shortcomings, keep his own score, with no one to blame but himself. By his early twenties Bill Hayes was back in the U.S., a rising star among pro golfers. But one day, in a matter of seconds, all his dreams came crashing down. A freak accident injured his spine, ending his golfing career forever.

His dreams now shattered, Bill had to start over. To pay for college he became a security guard at a juvenile detention center. Bill Hayes was left with nothing but painful memories, a prison full of delinquent teenagers, and one other thing—a spark that can only be defined as God quietly at work in his life. Bill had an idea. Drawing on his own experience as a young golfer, it occurred to Bill that perhaps what the boys in the prison needed was nothing more than a golfing lesson.

Bill Hayes taught the boys in the prison how to golf. He told them it was their own responsibility to face their shortcomings and keep score. The golf skills strangely empowered the boys. They began to think they were capable of learning other things. Bill was so inspired by the change he saw in them he decided to create a school for the disadvantaged. He would build the school on a golf course and use the lessons of the game to mold young people whose hearts and minds had been hardened by a violent world. He found a sympathetic ear in a man who was happy to lend his name to Bill's cause, the great golfer, Chi Chi Rodriquez.

13

Today, in Clearwater, Florida, stands the only public school in the world that exists on a golf course—The Chi Chi Rodriquez Youth Foundation. In 1992, after seeing hundreds of graduates from his program, Bill Hayes received the 758th Point of Light from President Bush for his work in education and with youth. Tiger Woods, Jack Nicklaus, Bobby Jones—there is much debate as to who is the most talented. But ask thousands of young people in Florida who the greatest golfer in the world is, and they won't hesitate for a moment. "The greatest golfer in the world— that's Bill Hayes."

—Eric Snyder for Rick Rusaw

What dreams in your life have been shattered by something unexpected? How did you react to the loss of those dreams?

How might God use your dream in a different way, to be an encouragement to others, just like he did with Bill Hayes?

_____

_____

_____

_____

_____

_____

_____

_____

_____

_____

_____

_____

Dr. Doom's Freefall

I do not understand what I do. For what I want to do I do not do,
but what I hate I do. . . . What a wretched man I am! Who will
rescue me from this body of death? Thanks be to God—through
Jesus Christ our Lord!

ROMANS 7:15, 24, 25

DR. DOOM'S FREEFALL

Long ago on a family vacation, my sons and I were in line for a
ride at Universal Studios Islands of Adventure. It was the kind
of ride I really don't like. First, anything with the name "Dr.
Doom's Freefall" doesn't sound like a good time to me. It calls
for you to allow yourself to be strapped into a seat that rockets
you in the air 150 feet and then forces you down faster than
gravity. Well, that just seems foolish.

I realize some people love those kinds of rides but I have never
been one of them. My reason for being in that line was a "dad
thing." I didn't want to look like a chicken with my teenage
sons. To make matters worse, I wasn't standing in line for Dr.
Doom's Freefall for the first time. I was there for the third time.
The first time I chickened out, using a cell phone call as a wonderful excuse to skip the ride. The second time there was no
convenient excuse to skip out, so with heart pounding and
palms sweating, I climbed aboard, grateful I hadn't passed out
from fear.

We'll do things we don't like for a good cause. That would
explain my riding Dr Doom's Freefall once. But a second time—
that could only have been a case of temporary insanity. As we
approached our turn to ride, I said to my sons, "I can't believe
I am doing this again—I hate this stuff." My son, Eric, said with
a big grin and bigger wisdom, "Isn't that how it goes? We love
the things we hate."

Eric's right. Dr. Doom's Freefall was something I hated and wanted at the same time. The Bible talks about that. It says, "I don't understand what I do. For what I want to do I do not do, but what I hate I do." We've all been there. We have great intentions. We know intuitively what's right. We decide we aren't going to make old mistakes again; but then . . .

Jesus understood the contradictions we live. In fact, his reason for coming to Earth was to reconcile the creation to the creator— to make right what had been broken within us, to recreate our nature, to repair the hole in our hearts, and to restore our souls.

I've spent enough of my life in line for Dr. Doom's Freefall, doing what I hate to do. Fortunately, Jesus has provided another way for me to live. He says it's good to take risks, but a different kind of risk than a crazy amusement park ride. His teaching tells us, "Love your neighbor. Do an act of kindness for a total stranger. Instead of building up riches on Earth, store up riches in Heaven. Live like that and you'll have the ride of your life."

—Rick Rusaw

What things do you hate and yet do anyway, again and again?
Why do you think this happens?

What would happen if you trusted Jesus to help you live differently? Write out a prayer, asking him to help you take risks that will please him, and to be able to give up doing the things you hate.

Why Ask Why?

O Lord, you are our Father.

    We are the clay, you are the potter;

    we are all the work of your hand.

ISAIAH 64:8

WHY ASK WHY?

You probably won't recognize his name, but Gustav Mahler was one of the world's greatest music conductors, even though he is now most often remembered for his compositions. I must admit that I had been acquainted with his music for some time without knowing much about him. I can't say the same now. His life journey has come to hold a bit of fascination for me as I have discovered this somewhat tragic figure of music history. He was born in Austria in 1860 and died in Vienna in 1911, and in those 51 years his life would be characterized by a constant struggle with many unanswered questions in his mind and heart. I think some of them will sound very familiar and, no surprise here, most of them have to do with difficulty, and they begin with the word "Why?"

Although he died almost 100 years ago, Mahler struggled with some questions in his life that are all too familiar to us today. Mahler would spend many years asking why he had experienced such a difficult childhood. He had a domineering father who struggled to make a living running a distillery and a mother who had married very much against her will. Of 14 children born to the family, only seven would survive infancy, and Mahler's next younger brother, his closest companion, would die prematurely, leaving him isolated and alone. He was a witness to his father abusing his mother and, at the age of five, when asked what he wanted to be when he grew up, he replied, "A martyr."

He struggled with relationships. He exhibited bizarre, unpredictable mood swings in the course of a conversation. He walked with a strange, almost spasmodic gait that some speculate may have been an emotional contact point with his disabled mother. He struggled with the "why" of such idiosyncrasies.

And there were many other "whys." Why was his music not any more popular or well-received? If his love was composition, why was he thrust into the world of conducting? Why did he feel so alone?

The apostle Paul would write a powerful letter to his Christian friends in Rome. This is what I take away from Romans 9:14–21:

> God has the first word, initiating the action in which we play our part for good or ill. Are you going to object, "So how can God blame us for anything since he's in charge of everything? If the big decisions are already made, what say do we have in it?" Who in the world do you think you are to second-guess God? Do you for one moment suppose any of us knows enough to call God into question? Clay doesn't talk back to the fingers that mold it saying, "Why did you shape me like this?" Isn't it obvious that a potter has a perfect right to shape one lump of clay into a vase for holding flowers and another into a pot for cooking beans?

Allow me to encourage you not to spend so much time trying to figure everything out. Mahler, a composer and musical genius, never did get answers to many of his questions, and you probably won't either. So, instead of asking God, "Why did you make me the way I am?" try asking, as an alternative, "What can I do for you?" The answers to that question will make life worth living.

—Dan Stuecher

25

List some of the things you wish you could change about yourself.

_____

_____

_____

_____

_____

_____

_____

_____

_____

_____

_____

_____

_____

_____

Knowing that God shaped you the way you are for a reason, how might he use those things you dislike about yourself for his glory?

_____

_____

_____

_____

_____

_____

27

_____

_____

_____

_____

_____

_____

_____

Box Brown

Be strong and courageous. Do not be terrified; do not be discouraged,

for the LORD your God will be with you wherever you go.

JOSHUA 1:9

BOX BROWN

Many of life's major victories are won at the cliff edge where courage and fear come together. Fear alone can be a cruel captor. Courage that moves ahead in spite of fear can be a great liberator. No one knew that better than Henry Brown.

Brown was a slave in Richmond, Virginia, in the 19th century. He had been separated from his family, and he slowly realized that if he remained a slave, he would die. He was terrified, but he knew he had to escape. The question was how. Brown was aware that the conventional routes to freedom in the northern states were no longer safe. Too many escaping slaves had been discovered by the authorities and returned to their owners. But Brown would not be deterred. He believed the words of Napoleon: "He who fears being conquered is sure of defeat." Though his plan was untried, Brown prayed he would succeed.

Brown cautiously approached Samuel Smith for assistance, a sympathetic businessman who regularly shipped large objects. Smith helped Brown build a box 2' 8" deep, 2' wide, and 3' long, with three small holes for fresh air. Armed with a container filled with water and a few biscuits, Brown was nailed into the box and shipped to William Johnson in Philadelphia, Pennsylvania. Though the outside of the box was stamped "This Side Up," Brown was placed on his head twice during the 27-hour trip north. While upside down, he had a hard time breathing and thought he would die. In the midst of terrible fear, nailed into a tiny box, Brown prayed that God would give him courage, help him overcome his fear, and deliver him from evil.

Brown's box was finally delivered to Philadelphia at 3:00 A.M. the day after it was shipped. Unfortunately for Brown, the box wasn't picked up for delivery to William Johnson's house for three more hours. But finally, after 30 hours in a tiny box (and sometimes on his head), Brown heard rapping and a voice ask, "Is all right within?" to which he replied, "All right."

The box was opened, and upon being freed, Brown broke into a song of deliverance and praise to God: "My labor was accomplished, my warfare was ended and I stood erect before my equal fellow men, a slave no more," he said.

Henry "Box" Brown, as he became known, was a man focused on the freedom beyond his fear. And freedom won. Remember, courage is not the absence of fear. Courage without fear is stupidity. Courage is moving forward in spite of the fear. For Box Brown, it meant the difference between life and death, and life won.

—Myron Williams for Paul S. Williams

What fears are holding you back from true freedom in your life?

_____

_____

_____

_____

_____

_____

_____

_____

_____

_____

_____

_____

Lift up your specific fears to God, asking for his strength and courage to move past them into his freedom.

_____

_____

_____

_____

_____

_____

33

_____

_____

_____

_____

_____

_____

_____

Do You Want to Get Well?

No discipline seems pleasant at the time, but painful. Later on,
however, it produces a harvest of righteousness and peace for those
who have been trained by it. Therefore, strengthen your feeble arms
and weak knees. "Make level paths for your feet," so that the lame
may not be disabled, but rather healed.

HEBREWS 12:11–13

DO YOU WANT TO GET WELL?

Jesus and his friends came upon a place called the Pool of Bethesda (see John 5:1–15). It was located near one of the gates into Jerusalem. This pool was known as a place of healing— that's why we have hospitals named Bethesda today. Legend had it that when the water stirred, the first person into the pool would be healed of his or her infirmities.

On a typical day it was possible to have a few hundred people waiting around the Pool of Bethesda. But on the day Jesus and his disciples visited the pool, one of those people had an experience he never forgot.

Jesus encountered a man the Bible tells us had been disabled for 38 years. Jesus asked him what seems to be a rather odd question, "Do you want to get well?" It was actually a pretty rude question. Of course, the guy wanted to be well! Why else would he have been by that pool? And who was this able-bodied man, Jesus, to suggest that someone might not want to get well?

I meet people all the time who say they want to get well. "I want my life to be better." "I want my marriage to improve." "I don't want to be so angry." "I don't want to be stuck." "I want to be well." But after more than 20 years in the people business, I catch myself wondering, "Do they *really* want to get well?" Frankly, many people get so comfortable in their failures that they don't want to do what it takes to get well.

When Jesus asked the disabled man at the Pool of Bethesda if he wanted to get well, his question wasn't meant to be rude or offensive. It was a great question. He knew if this man were going to be well, his whole world would change. The people and the relationships he had cultivated would change. The lifestyle he had gotten accustomed to would change. Being well meant that things were going to be different.

Many of us have grown accustomed to our infirmities, whatever they may be. We have learned to live with them. But Jesus invites us to change, to be well. It is a choice we get to make, a choice only we can make, by giving ourselves over to the healer. Jesus healed the disabled man, and his world changed in ways he had never imagined. Are you ready for your world to change? Do you want to get well?

—Rick Rusaw

What failures and struggles have your learned to live with? Have you actually become so comfortable in them that you don't want to change?

_____

_____

_____

_____

_____

_____

_____

_____

_____

_____

_____

_____

_____

What would it mean to give those struggles up to God and allow him to heal you? Sometimes healing is painful—are you prepared to go through the pain to reach wholeness again?

_____

_____

_____

_____

_____

_____

_____

_____

_____

_____

_____

Lessons from a Potted Plant

I will build [my people] up and not tear them down; I will plant

them and not uproot them. I will give them a heart to know me,

that I am the LORD. They will be my people, and I will be their God.

JEREMIAH 24:6, 7

LESSONS FROM A POTTED PLANT

We can learn from looking at nature. A young man's life was
once changed when he studied nature. His name was Uchimura
Kanzo. You've probably never heard of him. Born in Japan in the
mid-nineteenth century, Kanzo was part of the elite samurai class.
This gave him access to an education that taught him English.
One day he came across some Christian writings that influenced
him greatly. It wasn't long afterward that he decided to become
a follower of Christ. In 1885 he traveled to the United States in
search of a theological education. While attending seminary in
New England he became disillusioned with people in the
church, with the huge cultural differences between the East and
West, and most of all, with himself. He was painfully aware of
his own failures and felt as if his spiritual growth had become
completely stagnant. Then a friend pointed him in the direction
of something very revealing—a potted plant.

Uchimura Kanzo gained worldwide recognition in the late 1800s
for his work with the poor and the handicapped. His writings
influenced many in Japan, including some of the country's most
famous citizens. He authored 357 publications and was outspo-
ken against his government's warlike policies. For many years
he held weekly meetings in Tokyo where he typically spoke to
congregations of 500 to 700 people. He became involved in
environmental causes and was helpful in assisting the medical
work of Dr. Albert Schweitzer in Africa. And Kanzo would not
have accomplished any of this if not for one sad day while he
was a student in the United States. He was about to abandon his
faith until a college president used a potted plant to teach Kanzo
a valuable lesson.

When a farmer puts a seed into the ground, he can't see what's going on beneath the surface. He has to trust that the seed and the ground are doing what they're supposed to do and that someday there will be a crop to harvest. If the farmer spent all his time worrying about what's going on underground, he would be neglecting all the other things essential to the farm.

The president of the college took Kanzo aside and said, "It's not enough to look within yourself. Look beyond yourself, outside of yourself. . . . Look to Jesus, who redeemed your sins on the cross. What you are doing is like a child with a potted plant, who pulls up the plant to look at the roots to see if it is growing to his satisfaction. Why don't you trust everything to God and accept your growth as it occurs?" These words freed Kanzo to take his eyes off himself and look to the needs of others instead. As a result, not only did *he* grow spiritually, but the world did as well.

—Eric Snyder for Rick Rusaw

43

How do you feel about your spiritual growth right now? Are you constantly worrying about the progress of your "roots"?

_____

_____

_____

_____

_____

_____

_____

_____

_____

_____

_____

_____

How might your feelings change if you stopped worrying and started trusting God for your growth? Ask God today to help you look to him for the strength you need.

_____

_____

_____

_____

_____

_____

_____

_____

_____

_____

_____

_____

Life As a Princess

God demonstrates his own love for us in this: While we were still sinners, Christ died for us.

ROMANS 5:8

LIFE AS A PRINCESS

My youngest daughter, Jana, is a beautiful young woman in her early twenties. As is often the case with a youngest child, she loves to have fun and be the center of attention. Jana has a winter coat with the word *Princess* across the back in big, bold, white letters. A doorknob cover on her bedroom door says Princess. In her closet are blue, white, and pink shirts with PRINCESS, all in caps, across the front. No doubt about it, from the time she was a little thing, Jana saw herself as a princess.

But Jana came to me around the time of her 21st birthday and said "Pappy, I've discovered a terrible thing. I've learned the universe doesn't revolve around me." While she spoke the words in jest, the tone in her voice indicated an important truth had, in fact, been internalized. It was time to give up her princess title and move on to accept the realities of life.

Jana came to see that the question is not whether life meets our demands or not. The question is, will we meet life's demands? I was pretty pleased Jana was able to figure that out at 21 years of age. It takes most people considerably longer to realize we're here to serve, not to be served.

At whatever age we finally learn the difficult lesson, it is a blow to our fragile egos. I am not the center of the universe. The world doesn't exist to serve me. I am one of six billion living souls, and I'd better get used to the idea that I'm not all that special.

Or am I?

There was, in fact, one moment in all of human history when I was the center of the universe. I was the only thing that mattered.

I believe the story of Christ explains all of life, not only for me, but for all of us. And I believe the center of that story lies in one single event—the moment that Jesus, who had never done anything wrong in his life, died on the cross in my place. The worst suffering of all time happened there. And the wonderful, heart-breaking truth is that he would have chosen that death on the cross, even if I were the only other person in the world ever to have lived. He did it for me, for my one solitary life. And he did it for you too.

49

With that in mind I have to rethink what Jana said. Maybe she's not right after all. Maybe she is, in fact, the center of the universe. She always has been and always will be. After all, given the sacrifice he was willing to make on her behalf, none other than Jesus of Nazareth seemed to think so.

—Paul S. Williams

If you are a believer in Christ, then you truly are a prince or princess, for you are a child of the king of the universe. Give that idea some deep thought and write down your thoughts and feelings.

How does it feel to know that Jesus would die for you alone?

_____

_____

_____

_____

_____

_____

_____

_____

_____

_____

_____

_____

_____

Gideon

I do not trust in my bow,

  my sword does not bring me victory;

but you give us victory over our enemies,

  you put our adversaries to shame.

In God we make our boast all day long,

  and we will praise your name forever.

PSALM 44:6–8

GIDEON

I'm glad my parents didn't name me Gideon. Greg draws much less attention. In the Bible, Gideon gained the attention of God Almighty when he took part in an historic event of grand proportions (see Judges 7).

Gideon was the leader of an army who faced an enemy of great military strength—an army as thick as locusts, the Bible says— and could no more be counted than the sands of the seashore. There were probably hundreds of thousands of men. And Gideon's army? All he had were 32,000—a tiny fraction of the enemy's camp. And just as Gideon was rallying his troops for battle, God told Gideon to take 10,000 men out of his army. That's right. With the odds already stacked against him, God wanted Gideon to send 10,000 of his own men home. Gideon was shocked. It would be a bloodbath. But wait. God wasn't finished yet.

Before Gideon had gotten over the shock of that, God told him to take away 21,700 more! God left Gideon with only 300 men—300 soldiers to fight hundreds of thousands of enemy troops. But Gideon obeyed God, and those 300 men blew their trumpets and shouted "a sword for the LORD and for Gideon." And what happened? Those enemy soldiers actually turned their swords on each other. And mighty as that army had been, Gideon and his 300 men were triumphant. Against unbelievable odds, Gideon defeated the greatest army he had ever faced.

But why in the world had God asked Gideon to trim down his troops by 31,700 people? Why strip the army to bare bones?

God told us the answer in verse 2. God told Gideon that he didn't want his fighting men to boast that it was their own strength that had saved them and won the battle. He wanted the odds to be so terrible that there could only be one explanation for the victory—God himself.

Place your trust anywhere else, and the odds are against you. Place your trust in God, and no matter how bad the odds look to those on the outside, there is little doubt about the outcome.

—Greg Allen

55

What God-size challenge are you facing? Are you trusting your own resources to accomplish it or are you looking to God for the victory?

_____

_____

_____

_____

_____

_____

_____

_____

_____

_____

_____

_____

_____

How might God be asking you to cut the size of your "army" so that he can receive the glory?

A Secret Agony

*You intended to harm me, but God intended it for good to
accomplish what is now being done, the saving of many lives.*

GENESIS 50:20

A SECRET AGONY

As we grow old we tend to forget some things. And yet, with age, there are some things that become more vivid. The most productive years of life begin to fade from our memory, while our childhood becomes clearer. Maybe the increased dependence and helplessness of old age stir up familiar feelings from our youth. Near the end of his life, the Old Testament patriarch, Jacob, despite his prosperity, cried out in agony, "Everything is against me!" (Genesis 42:36).

"Boz" was the name of an English writer who, in his old age, felt very much the same way. He, like Jacob, was driven by his aspirations to achieve great and lasting success. But neither he nor Jacob ever conquered the pain inflicted by one of his own parents.

Jacob's father, Isaac, saw much promise in his son—his son Esau, that is. Esau was the brave hunter and adventurer. Jacob, on the other hand, was a shy homebody. Isaac invested himself in Esau's potential. He invested much less in Jacob. If he was to become anything, Jacob felt he was on his own. Boz knew how Jacob felt.

The year was 1824 and Boz was a small and weakly 12-year-old. His parents were poor and able to pay for only one child's education, and Boz was not the chosen one. They instead sent him to work in a rat-infested shoe polish factory where he, they imagined, would spend the rest of his life. Boz, like Jacob, felt he was on his own. In his later years he confided, "No words could express the secret agony of my soul. . . . My whole nature was so penetrated with grief and humiliation, that even now, I often forget in my dreams that I am a man, and I wander desolately back to that time of my life." From the perspective of both Jacob and Boz, everything *did* seem to be against them.

Jacob thought God was against him. He was right. For it was God himself who changed Jacob's name to Israel, which means in Hebrew, "he struggles with God" (Genesis 32:28). But it was also God who made it very clear that it was "Jacob I loved" (Romans 9:13).

61

Boz's name changed as well. The characters and experiences of his boyhood poverty fueled his ability to write. He soon dropped the pseudonym "Boz" in exchange for his real name, Charles Dickens.

Good things came to both Jacob and Charles Dickens. But even in their old age, both remembered the pain of youth. Even when this life does eventually work out, it doesn't erase the pain of the past. For that, we'll have to wait for what lies on the other side. But for now, we can find joy in the good that God can bring out of our secret agony.

—Eric Snyder for Paul S. Williams

What hurts from your past still haunt you? Pour them out to
God here.

Look again at those hurts. How has God used those wounds to bring you and others greater good?

_____

_____

_____

_____

_____

_____

_____

_____

_____

_____

_____

_____

Old Bits of String

Get rid of all bitterness, rage and anger, brawling and slander,
along with every form of malice. Be kind and compassionate to
one another, forgiving each other, just as in Christ God forgave you.
Be imitators of God, therefore, as dearly loved children.

EPHESIANS 4:31–5:1

OLD BITS OF STRING

My wife's grandmother was a strong-willed woman who hated
to give up anything. She didn't want to move; she had lived in
the same farmhouse in Illinois for nearly all of her days. She
had been raised there, and she raised her own family under the
same old tin roof. But now she was unable to care for herself,
and she had no choice but to give up her home. After she was
settled into her senior apartment, the "old folks' home" (as she
called it), her family gathered at the farm to sort through all
those years of accumulation and to auction off the remaining
odds and ends. Lots of memories were found in the old closets
and the spare room—a whole life was contained in that country
farmhouse. The cupboards housed all the pots and pans she'd
cooked those great country meals in. The worn desk where she
had handwritten her articles for the local county newspaper sat
in the corner.

In the kitchen pantry the family discovered a paper sack. Inside
the sack were hundreds and hundreds of bits of string—tiny bits
of string with no apparent use. The bag containing the strings
was labeled "Strings too short to save." That's right, Grandma
had saved countless bits of string for which no practical use
could be found—a whole grocery bag full of them. Now what
would possess someone to save bits of string in a grocery bag
and then label the bag "Strings too short to save"?

We had a good laugh over Grandma's bag of string. She lived through the Depression, and that experience made her inclined to hang on to anything she thought might be needed if she came upon hard times again. But a bag labeled, "Strings too short to save"? We all had to agree that Grandma had gone a bit over the edge with that one.

But then, who am I kidding? I hang on to useless stuff all the time in the storehouse of my life. Regrets and grudges, remembered slights and petty omissions—I label them all "Stuff too petty to save." But I save them, nevertheless. Stubbornly I hang on to every last piece.

Who knows, maybe someday my kids will gather with their own children and talk about the stuff I've accumulated. I wonder what sack of useless stuff they will find tucked away in my pantry. It is easy to laugh when it's somebody else's bag of string.

—Rick Rusaw

67

What "old bits of string" are you hanging on to? Why?

_____

_____

_____

_____

_____

_____

_____

_____

_____

_____

_____

_____

_____

_____

What difference would it make in your life if you threw those
things out? How might it change your relationships with others
and with God?

_____

_____

_____

_____

_____

69

_____

_____

_____

_____

_____

_____

_____

_____

Having It All

Whoever wants to save his life will lose it, but whoever loses his life for me and for the gospel will save it. What good is it for a man to gain the whole world, yet forfeit his soul?

MαΓK 8:35, 36

HAVING IT ALL

"Why settle for less when you can have it all?" Throughout most of my life that question has had a worldly connotation to it, representative of a preoccupation with things that can't last, a restlessness of greed contrasting to the much more desirable calm of contentment. I have observed those who personify it, and they have almost always been very unsettled people, never able to enjoy much of anything for very long because something more was always out there somewhere, calling to them.

But it occurs to me that from a spiritual perspective the question makes a world of sense. "Why, indeed, would you want to settle for temporary things in this life when you can have the boundless wealth of eternity?" Why would anyone want to be preoccupied with what he can't keep at the expense of what otherwise would be his to possess forever?

The last few years in the life of the musical genius Gustav Mahler illustrate for us the futility of the worldly perspective of the question and consequently, also bring into sharp focus the power of its spiritual meaning. "Why settle for less when you can have it all?"

In the opening years of the twentieth century, Vienna, Austria, was the music capital of the world. There could be no more prestigious achievement for a seasoned musician than to be Principal Conductor and Director of the great Viennese Imperial Opera. At 37 years of age, Gustav Mahler would ascend to that pinnacle in the rarefied atmosphere of the world's musical elite. It had been a consuming dream and goal for most of his adult life. His name was now known internationally. Demand for performances of his music was at a fever pitch all over Europe. He had arrived! He could easily have asked, "Why settle for less when you can have it all?"

72

However, after devoting 10 years of his life to the opera, Mahler would finally conclude that what he had seen as "all" was, in reality, a great deal "less." His beloved 4-year-old daughter would die of diphtheria; his marriage would grow unstable from the shock; his health would shatter; friends would turn against him; subordinates would thwart his leadership; and he would eventually leave a symphony unfinished. He finally resigned the position he had coveted most of his life. Suddenly, the question had become, "Why settle for having it all, if it's going to cost you everything?"

Even before he died, Mahler experienced what death eventually does to the rest of us. It strips us of every earthly possession, ignites explosive questions about why our lives were lived in the first place, and confronts us with what, up to that point, had only been a fuzzy concept: destiny.

When Mahler's approaching death became a reality he could no longer ignore, it crumbled the foundations of everything he had thought was important. Although hundreds would attend his funeral in the driving rain of a thunderstorm, Mahler died alone, disillusioned, confused, and empty.

Jesus said, "Seek first his kingdom and his righteousness, and all these things will be given to you as well" (Matthew 6:33). Reflecting on the life of Mahler (and of most people for that matter), I have to ask, "Why settle for less when you can have it all?"

—Dan Stuecher

List some of the goals you are actively pursuing. Are they of temporary value or eternal worth?

_____

_____

_____

_____

_____

_____

_____

_____

_____

_____

_____

_____

In light of the list you just made, are there changes you need to make in the focus of your life's pursuits?

_____

_____

_____

_____

_____

_____

_____

_____

_____

_____

_____

_____

_____

75

Free to Fail

Trust in the LORD with all your heart

    and lean not on your own understanding;

in all your ways acknowledge him,

    and he will make your paths straight.

PROVERBS 3:5, 6

FREE TO FAIL

What would you do if you knew you could not fail? Would you set out to find a cure for cancer? Would you climb Mount Everest? Would you pull those long-forgotten dreams from the back of your childhood closet and let them see the light of day? It's interesting to think about, but the truth is there are no guarantees against failure. And sadly, the fear of failure often stops us from fully embracing life.

Until we are free to fail we are never free to succeed. Unless we are open to the possibility of failure, we remain closed to the opportunity for success.

When my three children were infants, I enjoyed watching them develop their motor skills. Crawling came pretty easy to all three. Come to think of it, they all learned to sit up and even stand while holding onto the couch rather easily as well. But that's where the easy stuff ended, because the next challenge was to take a step alone. No couch to hold on to. No daddy's hand to steady the way.

And do you know what happened when they tried to walk? They fell down—over and over again. All three of them. They fell down so often and so hard I was amazed they ever tried again. But try again they did, until they finally got it right. There was no self-consciousness, no fear that everyone was watching, no concern that they weren't walking as quickly as their friends. They felt completely and utterly free to fail. And in that freedom was the secret to their success.

Jesus received word that his good friend Lazarus was sick and about to die (see John 11). Lazarus's family wanted Jesus to come. But they were in Judea, and there was a good chance Jesus would be killed if he traveled into Judea. But Jesus decided to go anyway, and his disciples were very reluctant to follow. They did not want to take that first step. They thought they would all be killed.

But then one of the disciples, Thomas, remembered the truth: *We'll never be free to succeed until we're free to fail.* And he said to the others, "Let us also go, that we may die with him." And with that they all found the courage to take the first step, in spite of possible failure. They followed Jesus into Judea and no one was killed. In fact, the opposite happened—Jesus raised Lazarus from the dead—a success far beyond anything they ever could have imagined.

But note, the disciples would not have seen Lazarus's resurrection if they hadn't been willing to let go and take that first step. There is only one decent way to live this life, full of fear and failure as it is, and that is to trust Jesus and take that first step forward.

—Rick Rusaw

What would you do if you knew you couldn't fail? Are you willing to try even if you might fail, trusting Jesus and taking a step of faith?

_____

_____

_____

_____

_____

_____

_____

_____

_____

_____

_____

_____

What is the worst that could happen if you do fail? On the other hand, what might happen if you succeed?

_____

_____

_____

_____

_____

_____

_____

_____

_____

_____

_____

_____

_____

_____

Homemade Dressing

Enter his gates with thanksgiving

and his courts with praise;

give thanks to him and praise his name.

For the LORD is good and his love endures forever;

his faithfulness continues through all generations.

PSALM 100:4, 5

HOMEMADE DRESSING

Even before I walked in the front door I could smell it—homemade biscuit dressing (stuffing). At Thanksgiving we were always at Grandma's house in the country. The little white house sat nestled on the 66-acre farm in Big Clifty, Kentucky, and the homemade dressing smelled perfect in Grandma's kitchen. She started early in the morning, making homemade biscuits while the turkey roasted in the oven. Every now and then she'd add a little turkey juice to a big old bowl where her secret dressing recipe came to life. Thanksgiving dinner consisted of garden-grown everything that covered an entire table. But even with all that food, it was the dressing I remember. Not even caramel cake, apple pie, or homemade ice cream competed with Grandma's homemade biscuit dressing. That very simple but delectable memory belongs to me today because of Grandma's hard work years ago. And so it is with Thanksgiving.

All of us enjoy Thanksgiving dinner today because centuries before my grandmother was born a group of Puritans sought out religious freedom by sailing to a brave new world. But we forget how hard it was for those first Pilgrims to make it to that first Thanksgiving dinner. It took months of sailing which involved the tragic deaths of many loved ones. There must have been plenty of second-guessing before they ever even got to shore. And once they landed on their new frontier, they had to start their lives all over, from establishing a way to provide clean drinking water to electing leaders for a new government. Again there were months of hard work, family members dying, and more second-guessing the wisdom of their pilgrimage to this new land. But their hard work paid off, and little by little they came to see they were now free.

When I was in first grade, my elementary school made a big deal about Thanksgiving. I remember dressing up as a Pilgrim and going to a school function where everyone else was also dressed as Pilgrims—knickers with white socks and black shoes and those funny-looking hats. We'd walk around the school to see how each classroom portrayed Thanksgiving. I remember a lot of pumpkins, turkeys, and horns of plenty. As a little first grader I had no idea that the early Pilgrims gave up their homeland and security to come to America and risk death to establish the land of the free— no idea of the privilege it was to enjoy Thanksgiving. I'm not sure I fully understand that privilege now, but I want to. I want to be thankful for homemade dressing, horns of plenty, freedom to worship God, freedom to say the Pledge of Allegiance, and being called an American. I want to remember the sacrifice that brings the simple memories—and thanksgiving.

—Greg Allen

85

Name people who worked hard and went through difficult times to give you a good life. What trials did they go through?

_____

_____

_____

_____

_____

_____

_____

_____

_____

_____

_____

_____

_____

God sent his Son to go through the ultimate suffering to give us life and freedom. Write a prayer giving thanks for his sacrifice. Thank him too for those people in your life who sacrificed for you.

_____

_____

_____

_____

_____

_____

_____

_____

_____

_____

_____

Cracked Dishes

We are hard pressed on every side, but not crushed; perplexed,

but not in despair; persecuted, but not abandoned; struck down,

but not destroyed. We always carry around in our body the death

of Jesus, so that the life of Jesus may also be revealed in our body.

For we who are alive are always being given over to death for

Jesus' sake, so that his life may be revealed in our mortal body.

2 CORINTHIANS 4:8–11

CRACKED DISHES

Josephine Cochrane was 44 years old when her husband, a
wealthy merchant, died. She was used to living in luxury, and
suddenly all she had was $1,500 and a pile of debts. The year
was 1885, and the best a widow could hope for at that time was to
remarry. But Josephine didn't have much to offer a suitor,
especially in the "age and beauty" department. On top of all that,
by her own admission, she was a bit of a perfectionist. It used to
drive her crazy when her servants washed her fine china and
chipped an edge off of a cup or saucer. So here she was, no husband and no money—just a set of chipped dishes and one other
extremely valuable possession . . . an idea. Josephine's idea
would change the way millions of people lived, and what's more,
it would change Josephine.

At this point in her life, an idea and a set of china dishes were
all that Josephine had. She wanted to protect her dishes, which
had been in her family since the 17th century; but every time
they were washed by hand, she would find a chip or a crack. She
imagined that the safest way to clean them would be to somehow
aim water jets at the dishes while they were stabilized in a rack.
She came up with a design and began to work on her idea in a
shed behind her house. Josephine was no mechanic and was not
accustomed to working hard, but four years later she came out
of the shed and presented to the world her Garis-Cochrane
Dishwashing Machine.

We may never know why certain things happen. The script of our lives rarely plays out the way we would like. Tragedy and loss never seem to make sense. Josephine Cochrane had no control over her circumstances; she lost her husband, her status, and most of her possessions. But though the circumstances of life left her no choice, and she was able to choose how she would make her way in the world. And because of that choice she invented and marketed the first automatic dishwasher. She took the cracked dishes of her life and used them as an opportunity, instead of a liability.

Josephine Cochrane died a successful woman at the age of 74— leaving behind her invention and her successful company, the Kitchen Aid brand.

We may not live to see the end of our struggles or the fruit of our ideas like Josephine Cochrane did. But to live at all is to rise each day in the hope that somehow, in the whole scheme of things, what we do with our lives is going to make a difference in the unfolding of God's work on Earth.

—Eric Snyder for Rick Rusaw

What are your "cracked dishes"—things you didn't choose or
cause to happen, but that happened anyway?

_____

_____

_____

_____

_____

_____

_____

_____

_____

_____

_____

_____

Like Josephine, how can you look at your own cracked dishes as opportunities to make a difference in the world?

_____

_____

_____

_____

_____

_____

93

_____

_____

_____

_____

_____

_____

_____

Sheer Terror

In the sixth month, God sent the angel Gabriel to Nazareth, a town in Galilee, to a virgin pledged to be married to a man named Joseph, a descendant of David. The virgin's name was Mary. The angel went to her and said, "Greetings, you who are highly favored! The Lord is with you." Mary was greatly troubled at his words and wondered what kind of greeting this might be. But the angel said to her, "Do not be afraid, Mary, you have found favor with God. You will be with child and give birth to a son, and you are to give him the name Jesus. He will be great and will be called the Son of the Most High. The Lord God will give him the throne of his father David, and he will reign over the house of Jacob forever; his kingdom will never end."

LUKE 1:26–33

SHEER TERROR

Our son teaches fourth grade in Philadelphia. He is 25. It seems just yesterday he was an infant, nestled in his mother's arms, his face beet red, his bare chest beating too rapidly, a cool wash-cloth covering his forehead. His temperature was 105 degrees. We were young—too young—and terrified. The pediatrician met us at his office and saw three patients—our sick little boy and his two frightened parents. The doctor took care of us. We reluctantly left his office for a sleepless night at home with a sick infant. It was the first time I knew the sheer terror of parenting.

Years later my son called me on my office phone. He was a sophomore in college. I was ready for his typically confident voice, but as soon as he said, "Dad," I knew something was wrong. He started crying. Finally he choked out that things weren't going so well, and he was coming home. I hung up the phone and stared at the barren winter ground outside my office window. I drove to the school where his mother teaches, and called her out of class. I told her the news, as the children peered through the narrow glass on the classroom door. Again I knew how frightfully difficult parenting can be.

Now my son teaches 27 fourth-grade students in an inner-city public school classroom on the west side of Philadelphia. We are justifiably proud of him. But not far beneath the surface, tucked in the depths of my heart, is the frightening realization that it might not have turned out this way. Happy endings are not assured.

Gabriel, an ambassador of the realm, had seen his share of suffering. He watched soldiers die at the hands of the enemy. He knew of infants abandoned in the dead of night, with no hope of morning. He watched disease, famine, and hatred take the lives of thousands without blinking an eye. But he had never seen anything that terrified him as much as this. Not anything.

She was barely a child herself. And yet she had been chosen to bear the only hope the world would ever know. Bear hope in a hostile land, nurture it, and bring it to full flower. And as Gabriel brought the news to her, you couldn't help but notice the sheer terror in his voice, to understand that the future of the universe hung on shoulders as fragile as this young girl's. But he gave the message, heard her reply, and understood the truth. God has always done his most important work through fragile, broken vessels.

—Paul S. Williams

97

When have you felt sheer terror? How did you react?

_____

_____

_____

_____

_____

_____

_____

_____

_____

_____

_____

_____

_____

How do you think you would have felt and reacted if you were Mary, hearing Gabriel's announcement that you would bear the Son of God?

_____

_____

_____

_____

_____

99

_____

_____

_____

_____

_____

_____

_____

_____

Bitter or Better?

These [trials] have come so that your faith—of greater worth than gold, which perishes even though refined by fire—may be proved genuine and may result in praise, glory and honor when Jesus Christ is revealed.

1 PETER 1:7

BITTER OR BETTER?

Loss is one of life's greatest tests. We are often defined as people not by what we manage to hold on to, but by what we cannot keep. Whether it be relational, financial, or physical, loss demands a decision from us. Will we continue on, or will we fall back? Will we renew our commitment to the journey, or will we pack it in? Will we seize life, or be consumed by it?

These were the momentous issues forcing themselves on Ludwig van Beethoven in the summer of 1802. And what had he lost, this man who so many regard as the greatest composer to have ever lived? He had lost his hearing.

Beethoven was 32 years old. He was hitting his stride. Mozart had warned the music world they would be hearing great things from this young man. His music was strong, courageous, and passionate. But for some time he had known the day was approaching when he would not be able to hear a thing. In the summer of 1802 Beethoven packed his bags and, as he did almost every summer, escaped the heat of Vienna and indulged his love of nature by living in a small village in the countryside. As his hearing deteriorated, it would be during this summer that he would decide whether to go on or give up. His agony is evident in a letter he wrote to his brothers:

> O you who consider me as unfriendly, how greatly do you wrong me. For you do not know the secret reason why I appear to you to be so. Though endowed with a passionate and lively temperament and even fond of the distractions offered by society, I was soon obliged to seclude myself and live in solitude. I could not bring

myself to say to people: "Speak up, shout, for I am deaf."
How could I possibly claim the impairment of a sense,
which, in me, should be more perfectly developed than
in other people? I cannot do it; so forgive me, if you
see me withdrawing from your company, which I used
to enjoy. How humiliated I have felt if somebody
standing beside me heard the sound of a flute in the
distance and I heard nothing. I take leave of you and,
more sadly, the hope of being cured even to a certain
extent I must now abandon completely. Oh when,
Almighty God, shall I be able to hear?

Young Beethoven was truly driven to despair over losing his hearing. He even entertained thoughts of taking his life. He said that
the loss "made me despair, and I was on the point of putting an
end to my life—the only thing that held me back was my music."

Even on the verge of self-destruction, he knew that he had more
to give to this life. He would face this crisis head-on near the
end of that fateful summer. He would gain a remarkable resolve
that would equip him not merely to endure, but to assume a
maturity in his heart that would stimulate the greatest compositions of his life—most of them written when he could not hear a
single note.

Loss is a very much a test that insists on one of two responses.
We can allow it to make us bitter, or we can demand that it make
us better. The choice is ours and ours alone.

—Dan Stuecher

We all must face loss in our lives. What losses have you had to face?

_____

_____

_____

_____

_____

_____

_____

_____

_____

_____

_____

_____

_____

_____

How have you responded to your losses? With bitterness? Or have you allowed them to make you stronger? Why have you responded this way?

_____

_____

_____

_____

_____

_____

_____

_____

_____

_____

_____

_____

_____

Mr. Goodyear's Accident

Perseverance must finish its work so that you may be mature and complete, not lacking anything.

James 1:4

MR. GOODYEAR'S ACCIDENT

If we have eyes to see, there are interesting stories behind ordinary things. Take rubber for instance. Rubber is in every tire on every vehicle, every electrical wire in every building, and every rubber band. The world uses 4.5 million tons of rubber annually. It's not a "stretch" to say that without rubber we're not going anywhere.

Joseph Priestly first called the fruit of what is now called the rubber tree "rubber" when he discovered it was good for "rubbing out" pencil mistakes. But the substance had a tendency to melt when it was too hot and break when it was too cold. And most people thought the gooey substance from the rubber tree was destined to be useless in a technological age. But then one man stumbled on information that changed the world. That man was Charles Goodyear.

Others may have given up on the gooey fruit of the rubber tree, but Goodyear kept on tinkering. On one occasion he took the rubber tree sap and accidentally got it mixed up with sulfur on a hot stove. His accident stabilized the rubber. Now it didn't melt in hot temperatures or break when it was cold. It was pliable yet resilient, strong yet cushioning. It wasn't long before Mr. Goodyear had earned himself and his offspring a tidy fortune, as well as an internationally recognized name.

A couple of decades ago a chemist at the 3M Company accidentally created a glue that was barely strong enough to hold anything
together. With the slightest of pulls, the glue would separate.
But instead of throwing the useless stuff down a trash bin, the
people at 3M invented a use for the "not very sticky" glue, and
the Post-it® note was born.

I wish I could count the number of times I've been stuck in my
life, when my plans weren't working out and my ideas seemed
worthless. But do you know what I've learned from Charles
Goodyear, the folks at 3M, and my own life experience? I've
learned that it often doesn't matter when your plans fall through
or your ideas fail. The important thing is to learn from your
mistakes and to try again. In the process you just might open
yourself up to a marvelous new world that God was waiting for
you to find all along.

—Eric Snyder for Rick Rusaw

What has you "stuck" right now? What plans have you made that have now fallen through? What mistakes have you made that have you feeling frustrated?

Think about your mistakes and disappointments. What can they teach you? What new directions will they cause you to take? How might God be using them to help you become a better person?

_____

_____

_____

_____

_____

_____

_____

_____

_____

_____

_____

_____

_____

Scars

He heals the brokenhearted

and binds up their wounds.

PSALM 147:3

SCARS

I was only 11 when it happened. It was in the woods of Liverpool, New York, where I was playing chase with my friends. I tripped and fell and landed on a piece of broken glass. The cut was long and deep, right across a small vein in the palm of my hand.

I am not good with blood. I am even worse when it's my own. I barely made it home without passing out. My mom took me to the emergency room, and 11 stitches later I was released. It isn't very often that I get back home to my old neighborhood, but when I do, I look at the scar on my hand, and remember the day I fell running in the woods and sliced open my skin on that piece of broken glass.

I am 43 now, and there are plenty of other scars I have managed to accumulate in life, each one with a story. As I recall the stories of some scars, the details are foggy. Others I remember in vivid detail. It is hard to live very long and avoid racking up scars. Some are my own fault. Others are just random. Some are quite visible. Others are very private. All of them were painful, and most took a long time to heal.

When I cut my hand, if I hadn't let the doctor do his work cleaning the cut and sewing the stitches, my hand would not have healed properly. If I had constantly picked at the wound, it would never have healed at all. But I let the doctor work on the wound, cleaning and suturing it, and then I left it alone until it healed, and now I have a scar. It doesn't hurt anymore, but every time I see that scar, I'm reminded of that day.

Of course, these physical injuries are not my only scars. There are some scars on my heart too. You probably have them as well. Maybe it's a bankruptcy, or a divorce, or alienation from a loved one. Those scars hurt horribly and then hurt again when God cleans the wounds and sutures them closed. There is no other choice though. Letting God work on the wounds is the only way to be healed.

I can still remember how much it hurt when I cut my hand and how painful it was again when I had the wound cleaned and sutured. But the wound is healed now, and it's all because I let the doctor do his work. And what about the wounds of your heart? God understands how much they hurt. But they can be healed too, if you'll let the great physician do his work. You'll still have the scar—but now it will be a reminder of a great healing that once took place.

—Rick Rusaw

List some of the hurts in your life right now. Are you holding on
to some of your wounds, afraid of the pain of allowing God to
heal you?

Write a prayer, telling God of your fear, and asking him to help you be open to his healing. Mention your hurts specifically. God will be faithful to gently heal your soul.

Ignatius of Loyola

I thank Christ Jesus our Lord, who has given me strength, that he considered me faithful, appointing me to his service. Even though I was once a blasphemer and a persecutor and a violent man, I was shown mercy because I acted in ignorance and unbelief. The grace of our Lord was poured out on me abundantly, along with the faith and love that are in Christ Jesus. Here is a trustworthy saying that deserves full acceptance: Christ Jesus came into the world to save sinners—of whom I am the worst. But for that very reason I was shown mercy so that in me, the worst of sinners, Christ Jesus might display his unlimited patience as an example for those who would believe on him and receive eternal life.

1 TIMOTHY 1:12–16

IGNATIUS OF LOYOLA

I am the youngest child in my family. I learned early to fight for attention. There were only two of us, though—my brother and me. I wonder what I'd have done if I had 12 brothers and sisters? Inigo de Loyola did.

Loyola was the last of 13 children born to a wealthy Spanish family in 1491. He was born in a province whose name could be translated as "to terrify the enemy." As you might imagine, there was a huge and legendary emphasis on fearlessness and aggressiveness among the region's men.

One of his brothers joined a ship's escort for Christopher Columbus and died heroically in the Spanish conquest of Naples. In fact, six of Loyola's seven older brothers became conquistadors or fighting men. No wonder, then, that he fantasized about a life of intrigue, gallantry, and knightly romance. He got into fights often and wanted to be a famous swordsman. He fell in love with the future queen of Portugal, and though thwarted in his desire to win her, by age 26 he was a macho swashbuckler, known for his charm.

But then came the first real battle of Loyola's life, and everything changed. In 1521, he found himself defending against the French offensive on the fortress in Pamplona. There were only a handful of men holding out against a highly trained French force of 300. Late in the nine-hour siege, an artillery shot shattered Loyola's right leg and injured the other. Soon after, the fortress surrendered and, to his surprise, Loyola found himself well cared for by the French conquerors. Back at home and still disabled from battle, Loyola began to read. He read stories of Christians who had expected their Christian faith to change their lives.

Loyola, like most others of his generation, was raised a Christian. But his nominal faith made no real difference in his life. His faith was a tree whose roots were parched. But as he read of others who felt the power of God pulsing through their veins, he developed a thirst, the likes of which he had never known before—a thirst to know God and feel his presence. And for the first time in his life, Loyola began to take his Christian faith seriously. He traveled to Jerusalem, studied for the priesthood in Paris, changed his name to Ignatius and was ordained in 1537.

In 1540 Ignatius Loyola sketched the formula for a society that would be designated by the name of Jesus—The Society of Jesus. A year later, the society was formed. And a rich boy from a province known for warriors became the founding leader of the Society of Jesus—the Jesuits. By 1626, just 85 years after its founding, there were 15,535 Jesuits with 56 seminaries, 44 novitiates, 234 houses and 443 colleges all over the world. Over the past 500 years it has been one of the most influential groups in all of Christendom—all because one man, recovering from battle wounds, decided finally and surely to commit himself to God, no matter what.

—Paul S. Williams

Have you ever decided to take Jesus seriously? Have you committed yourself to him? If you have, how has it changed your life? If you haven't, why not? What do you think is holding you back?

God changed a murderer named Saul into a passionate witness
for Jesus named Paul. He changed a brash young warrior named
Loyola into Ignatius, a father of the Christian church. How do
you want God to change you?

_____

_____

_____

_____

_____

123

_____

_____

_____

_____

_____

_____

The Shortest Route to Success

Commit to the LORD whatever you do,

and your plans will succeed.

The LORD works out everything for his own ends.

PROVERBS 16:3, 4

THE SHORTEST ROUTE TO SUCCESS

New York is the largest city in the United States, with a population of 7.3 million people. Its size is a symbol of American prosperity and greatness. The growth of the city on the east coast of the state can be traced back to the seed of an idea which was planted right here in western New York. The man who planted this seed at the turn of the 19th century did not intend to do so. The idea came to him, as great moments often do, during one of the most disappointing times in his life and in the most unlikely place.

Jesse Hawley was a simple man, a flour miller from the town of Geneva in western New York State. In the late 1700s Hawley had a shipment of flour, which would have paid off his creditors, had he been able to get it to market on time. Unfortunately he didn't, and he ended up in debtor's prison. There, with nothing but time on his hands, an idea struck him.

As he studied maps of the terrain and the rivers that flowed across the state of New York he devised a plan by which a canal could be dug from the Great Lakes to New York City. It would be the first super highway of the new country. Governor De Witt Clinton led the campaign to build the canal almost exactly to Hawley's plan. "Clinton's Ditch," as it came to be known, was successfully completed in 1825. The ease and speed of travel that resulted from the Erie Canal created a revolution in American prosperity, not only in material goods, but also in ideas.

We are indebted to Jesse Hawley's inability to pay *his* debts. Our lives, like his, may be full of unexpected delays and miserable disappointments. But given time we may discover that life's detours are in reality the shortest route to success.

The seed of a great idea, the Erie Canal, was planted in western New York State. Historians now credit the growth of New York City to it. The Abolitionist Movement and the Underground Railroad found their roots here. In fact the Union victory in the Civil War was dependent on the Erie Canal. The women's movement, with Elizabeth Cady Stanton and Susan B. Anthony, found success because of it. So did Clara Barton and the American Red Cross.

To be made in the image of God, full of creativity and possibility, even in the darkest of times, is a most marvelous thing. One of the greatest accomplishments of New York State was born deep within the unlikely walls of a lonely jail cell. It's not the first time God brought redemption into the middle of one man's failure, and it won't be the last.

—Eric Snyder for Rick Rusaw

127

Write and reflect on a time when you were forced to take a detour in life—when your plans were derailed and it seemed like nothing was going right.

What good things came out of that detour? Did you learn a valuable lesson? Did you end up with an even better outcome than you had planned?

_____

_____

_____

_____

_____

_____

_____

_____

_____

_____

_____

_____

A Rough Start

Though my father and mother forsake me,

the LORD will receive me.

Teach me your way, O LORD;

lead me in a straight path.

PSALM 27:10, 11

A ROUGH START

How much are your parents "to blame" for who you are and the problems you have today? We hear from people who think this way all the time, don't we? "My father never showed me any affection, and I'm an angry, conflicted man today because of it." "My parents couldn't get along and consequently I don't know how to maintain relationships." "I was abused as a child, and now I'm a wreck as an adult."

We all had our struggles growing up, but some definitely had more than others. Neglected, deprived, and abandoned children grow up struggling with problems that those of us who were reared in loving homes may never face. But what exactly is the connection between our upbringing and our individual responsibility to live life? Can we blame the past for our failures in meeting the challenges of the present?

A boy was born in a slum tenement building described by one visitor this way: "On entering it, it is difficult to repress a shiver of bewilderment and dismay." It was located in an area called "Adulterers' Walk," if that tells you anything. The marriage of his parents was one of convenience. She was a 41-year-old disabled person with distant attachments to wealthy society, and he was a 24-year-old vagabond looking for something in life to which he could be attached. Their courtship had lasted a week.

Such were the boy's parents. He grew up having absolutely no relationship with his older sister or his younger brother. For the most part, he was left to find his own way.

Would you guess I might be describing one who would become a social outcast, a criminal, or a drain on society? Would such a background propel this boy into an adult life of anger and disillusionment with no purpose or direction? Thankfully, for all of us, the boy's circumstances did the opposite for him.

The formative years were difficult for Johannes Brahms. But it would have been the same for most children living in the slums of Hamburg, Germany, in 1835. A ghetto would seem an unlikely place to nurture an aspiring young composer. But he would find his way to greatness. He would rub shoulders with the likes of Liszt, Schumann, Wagner, and Dvorak. People would compare him to his idol, Beethoven. Brahms would become the toast of Vienna, one of the most beloved composers of his era.

A rough start doesn't necessarily cause or dictate failure at the finish. Indeed, as would be the case in the lives of many other composers, the adversities of Brahms' young life would be the keys to unlock his creative genius.

Did his early life have any detrimental effect on him? Yes, of course. He had his idiosyncrasies. He smoked a box of cigars every day. He drank too much. His strange sense of humor expressed itself in a rocking chair rigged to collapse if an unsuspecting visitor chose to sit in it.

133

As a little boy he found great pleasure in playing with tin soldiers, a means of escape that he would carry over into the rest of his adult life. But he would emerge from a challenging upbringing and be remembered, not for a life of crime or rage or tragedy, but for music that has touched and inspired millions.

—Dan Stuecher

Did you have a rough start in life? Even the happiest childhood leaves some scars. What are yours?

_____

_____

_____

_____

_____

_____

_____

_____

_____

_____

_____

_____

Try looking at those scars from a different perspective: How have they made you stronger, more creative, or more compassionate?

Joe

May my vindication come from you;

    may your eyes see what is right.

Though you probe my heart and examine me at night,

    though you test me, you will find nothing;

    I have resolved that my mouth will not sin.

As for the deeds of men—

    by the word of your lips

I have kept myself

    from the ways of the violent.

My steps have held to your paths;

    my feet have not slipped.

I call on you, O God, for you will answer me;

    give ear to me and hear my prayer.

PSALM 17:2–6

JOE

Joe had a great job, but he lost it. He had great credibility, but he lost that too. Joe was the head groundskeeper for a Mr. Genes who owned Rapitop, a successful software company. Groundskeeper may mean nothing to you, but you have to understand that Mr. Genes's home included a finely manicured 21 acres of prime suburban real estate. As the head groundskeeper, Joe managed a staff of 12 and a budget of one million dollars a year. Mr. Genes loved Joe and paid him well. So how did Joe lose his job and his credibility?

Mr. Genes asked Joe to stay in the guesthouse while he was on a business trip. He felt it was good for the staff and safer for his wife to have someone on the premises. Joe took a short swim in the pool and headed to the guesthouse in his swim robe. As he reached for the door handle he noticed it was slightly open. He didn't worry but did wonder. He walked into his living room, and there was Mrs. Genes, also in a robe.

She propositioned Joe. And after Joe's one-minute argument of "How could I do this to my boss?" Mrs. Genes said the obvious, "No one will ever know." But as she grabbed Joe's robe, Joe ran, leaving his robe in her hands.

The rest is terrible. Although Joe was a man of character and noble action, Mrs. Genes accused him of inappropriate advances, and Joe was fired. That was the day Joe lost a great job and his credibility. Now where is the hope in that story? Where is the hope for a man who did the right thing?

The man Joe was actually Joseph in the Bible. The king of the land was Potiphar, and he thought the world of Joseph—a great worker of the highest character. One day Potiphar's wife tried to seduce Joseph (see Genesis 39). Joseph refused and said, "How could I do such a wicked thing and sin against God?" But Potiphar's wife persisted, and as she grabbed his robe, Joseph ran. But Potiphar's wife accused him of wrongdoing in order to cover up her own evil. Her husband believed her, and Joseph lost his job, his credibility, and his robe.

So where was the hope for Joseph? He did what was right and suffered terrible consequences. The hope is found after the story. The Bible goes on to tell us that, even though Joseph went to jail, the warden put him in charge of the other prisoners. Joseph found favor in the eyes of God, and so God gave him success in all he did. Success far beyond anything he ever could have imagined. He ended up the ruler over all of Egypt—because doing the right thing is always rewarded. Maybe not right away. Maybe not even in this life. But God's blessings will eventually flow to those whose hearts are always turned to him.

—Greg Allen

Have you ever been wrongly accused or put in a compromising position, through no fault of your own? How did you react? What was the outcome?

_____

_____

_____

_____

_____

_____

_____

_____

_____

_____

_____

_____

Read the story of Joseph and Potiphar's wife in Genesis. What can you learn from Joseph about living with integrity in difficult situations?

Fear

There is no fear in love. But perfect love drives out fear.

1 JOHN 4:18

FEAR

They still call him "The Master of Suspense." As a movie director, Alfred Hitchcock was remarkably gifted at making movies so frightening that people were held utterly spellbound. All 53 of his major productions were successful. He once observed, "Even my failures make money and become classics a year after I make them." Anyone else would be bragging, but Hitchcock was telling the truth. The secret to his huge success was his understanding of the mechanics of fear in the human mind and heart. Here's how he put it: "There is no terror in a bang, only in the anticipation of it."

Alfred Hitchcock made a career out of his profound understanding of a principle you and I most often fail to realize. Our anticipation of what we do not know or understand is often more frightening and destructive than the actual object of our fear.

144

How many times have you feared something that never even happened? Or if it did happen, could it be that you were pleasantly surprised to discover it wasn't nearly as bad as you had feared? I'm convinced there are people around us every day doing their best to avoid God in fearful anticipation of what they believe he might do. Although they might not admit it, they are afraid of him because they do not know him or understand him. In their ignorance, they are tragically terrorized by false assumptions, constantly evading, dodging, resisting and misinterpreting him as though he might zap them at any moment. The contrast between such anxiety and reality could be rather humorous if it weren't so sad. After all, this is the God who thought up, brought into existence, and is the embodiment what we call love.

It is one of those sentences that defines our nation's history: "The only thing we have to fear is fear itself." Franklin Roosevelt first made that powerful statement on March 4, 1933, regarding the economic panic facing America. Years later he would declare it again to reassure a nation going to war.

Roosevelt understood fear. His command of it would equip him to mobilize and lead a country through a crippling depression and, years later, to victory in a war for which we were sorely unprepared.

Alfred Hitchcock understood it. From his imaginative grasp of fear would come films that have kept millions of moviegoers on the edges of their seats.

And Jesus truly understood it. Because he knew God, because he understood God, and because he was God, he could say, "Do not let your hearts be troubled. Trust in God; trust also in me" (John 14:1).

—Jennifer Taylor for Dan Stuecher

145

What are your greatest fears? Have any of them been realized?
If so, was the reality as frightening as you anticipated it would be?

_____

_____

_____

_____

_____

_____

_____

_____

_____

_____

_____

_____

Are you afraid of God? Do you avoid him because you fear his anger? Why do you think you fear a God that gave up his life because he loved you?

_____

_____

_____

_____

_____

_____

_____

_____

_____

_____

_____

_____

_____

A Deadly Trick

God . . . has saved us and called us to a holy life—not because of
anything we have done but because of his own purpose and grace.
This grace was given us in Christ Jesus before the beginning of time,
but it has now been revealed through the appearing of our Savior,
Christ Jesus, who has destroyed death and has brought life and
immortality to light through the gospel.

2 TIMOTHY 1:8–10

A DEADLY TRICK

I've often been impressed that our lives either take on greater clarity of meaning or become the object of greater confusion the closer we come to the end of them. Because I am a minister and am often asked to officiate at funerals, I suppose I have a perspective that is a bit more focused. There rarely seems to be any middle ground with how people deal with this time of life. There is either a sense of hope rooted in the spiritual realities of eternity or, in the absence of a spiritual understanding, there is a sense of hopeless finality that leaves some people shaken to the core.

Interestingly, in the last six months of his troubled life, Wolfgang Amadeus Mozart would experience both extremes— a fascinating combination of events that raise a significant question for all of us.

150

The year was 1791, and Mozart was only 35 years old; but he was not well. In fact, this would be the last year of his difficult life. In July, his circumstances took a decided upswing. His wife, Constanze, gave birth to a second son. A newly completed opera premiered in Vienna and was met with huge success as the crowds continued to increase for its performances. A bitter enemy was reconciled as a friend. It seemed there would now be meaning to what had been a lifelong struggle for Mozart to gain fame, achieve even moderate material success, and sustain relationships. However, even as these developments lifted his spirits, a single incident in that same month of July would plunge him into depression and fear.

A tall, gaunt stranger dressed in gray would came calling that summer . . . many times. He did not identify himself and never would, but he left an anonymous letter with Mozart demanding that he write a requiem, or a composition for a funeral. Mozart was immediately distraught. Who was this? Why would he be told to write a requiem? Was he being told to write the music for his own funeral?

Even as he tried to enjoy the presence of his family, he was desperately consumed with composing *Requiem.* He gave one of his students instructions on how to finish it, increasingly fearful he would never be able to do so himself. The thought of his approaching death terrorized him. It need not have been so.

Mozart spent the last five months of his life in complete physical and mental breakdown. He was wracked by fever, hypertension, renal failure, and fainting spells. He suffered mental delusions that he was being poisoned. With all of this, he still worked frantically to complete the composition of funeral music an anonymous stranger had told him to write. Mozart was terrified of death. The sad truth of history is that he'd been set up. The ominous stranger was actually a hired agent of a nobleman who planned to steal the Requiem and pass it off as his own. It was a cruel trick life had played on the composer. But then, life plays tricks on us all.

151

We're tricked into thinking this is all there is. It is not. We're tricked into being frightened of death instead of understanding it is not the final word. We're tricked into believing the meaning of our existence is to grasp instead of to give.

I urge you not to fall prey to such trickery, but to stand confidently in the truth. God, our heavenly Father, has created us to be his children. We are adopted into his family through the sacrifice of his only Son who is the truth, so that we might enjoy his presence forever.

—Dan Stuecher

What do you think of death? Does the thought of it fill you with fear? Why or why not?

_____

_____

_____

_____

_____

_____

_____

_____

_____

_____

_____

_____

_____

Does knowing that you are a child of God and that he wants to be with you forever change your feelings about death? Why or why not?

_____

_____

_____

_____

_____

_____

_____

_____

_____

_____

_____

_____

_____

The Architect

We speak as men approved by God to be entrusted with the gospel.

We are not trying to please men but God, who tests our hearts.

1 THESSALONIANS 2:4

THE ARCHITECT

One of America's greatest architects was a man named Alfred B.
Mullet. After the Civil War, construction of federal buildings
exploded around the country. Mullet was the Supervising
Architect of the U.S. Treasury at the time. In 1874 alone, he
presided over the construction of 40 new buildings. His vision
and creativity brought dignity and praise to the buildings that
bear his mark. His last building, what is now called the Old
Executive Office Building, sits to the west of the White House.
This inspiring landmark is where the vice president works. It
also hosts many of Washington's most important diplomatic
events. It is a magnificent building. But oddly enough, it's also
the reason that two years after it was completed, Alfred B. Mullet
took his own life.

An architect expects the fruit of his labor to stand for generations
of people to behold, so a great amount of effort is put into the
design of a building. If the public does not respond well to the
design, it can be devastating to an architect's entire career. Take
the sad case of Alfred B. Mullet. Never mind that he had successfully presided over the construction of 40 Washington, D. C.,
buildings. It was his final building that meant the most to him.
That building took 17 years to complete. When it was finished it
was the largest office building in the United States. It was also
the most unique. Most Washington structures were designed
according to the Greek Revival style, but Mullet created his
building in the French Second Empire style. There was nothing
like it in the city.

Had Mullet lived he would have seen how respected the building became over the years. More than a thousand treaties have been signed there, including the Treaty of Versailles and the United Nations Declaration. But Mullet didn't get to see his building's glorious future. Instead, what took place upon the building's completion was devastating to the renowned architect.

When the Old Executive Office Building was completed, the building was opened to a thunderous round of—criticism. That's right, criticism. To say no one liked it would be an under-statement. Mark Twain called it "the ugliest building in America." The government refused to pay Mullet the $160,000 they owed him for the job. After two years of devastation brought on by the public response to his masterpiece, at the age of 56, Mullet took his own life.

Mullet didn't live to see the accolades, because his life was not rooted in anything richer than his own accomplishments. When our entire self-worth is tied up in what others think, then the tide of the times can drive us to despair.

Alfred Mullet's work needed to be tied to something deeper than public praise. It needed to be tied to something deeper than passing architectural trends. His work, like yours and mine, needed to be tied to the architect of all designs and all ages. His work needed to be tied to the architect of life itself. Because if we please that architect, no other opinions matter.

—Eric Snyder for Rick Rusaw

Whom are you most trying to please with your life? When people disapprove of you, how do you react?

How would your life be different if you sought to please God above pleasing people?

159

_____

_____

_____

_____

_____

_____

_____

_____

_____

_____

_____

_____

_____

Ambrose of Milan

Before I formed you in the womb I knew you,

before you were born I set you apart.

JEREMIAH 1:5

AMBROSE OF MILAN

For almost three decades I've been in ministry. But I've held other jobs too. I've been an adoption caseworker, a radio announcer, a musician, and a college professor. It always seemed as if a bunch of random events occurred that ended up taking me down some unexpected pathway. But as the years went by, I began to wonder. Just how random were those events? In fact, when I look back on my life, there seems to be a pattern through it all—it's as if my sails have been filled with a steady wind blowing where it wills. After decades of thinking I was in control of my life, I'm finally learning to relax, go with the wind, and enjoy the ride.

That's what happened to the governor of Milan, Italy, all the way back in A.D. 374. He suddenly found himself in a profession he never expected—and smack in the middle of God's will for his life. And it was the voice of a child that God used to put him there.

Ambrose was trying to prevent a riot. The archbishop had just died, and people were sharply divided over who should take his place. An angry crowd formed, and Governor Ambrose spoke to the people, begging them to behave like Christians. Suddenly a child spoke up from the crowd, and that child's words changed the life of the governor of Milan. The child said: "Ambrose, bishop."

There is some doubt as to whether Ambrose was even a Christian at this point in his life. But the little boy repeated the words, and the crowd started chanting along—"Ambrose—bishop. Bishop Ambrose." The people had spoken, and before long, so did the emperor.

An inexperienced Ambrose had, against his wishes, suddenly become the archbishop of Milan. To his surprise his law training had actually prepared him for the position. Knowing Greek and Latin, he began to study the Scriptures, which inspired devotion in him and convinced him that Jesus was God in the flesh. But Ambrose's beliefs about Jesus got him in considerable trouble. They were rather unpopular views with the emperor and his mother. Troops were sent to remove him from power.

Knowing the troops were coming, Ambrose did a strange thing. He drew the people together into the church, and they worshiped God. That's right. They worshiped. They read Scripture and sang hymns, and Ambrose preached. The troops refused to enter the church while worship was going on, and with the passing of time they were drawn into the worship themselves. The troops eventually left, and Ambrose remained the archbishop of Milan, growing in influence to become one of the greatest leaders in church history. All because a little child suggested a career he'd never thought about before.

So when the wind blows, hoist your sails. Read the wind and the water, and move in the direction you're prompted. Give up your conviction that you can be God, and be content to be guided by him instead. And above all, enjoy the ride. You never know where God might be leading you.

—Eric Snyder for Paul S. Williams

Think back on your life. Can you see a pattern that has led you to where you are today? Write about and reflect on the patterns you see.

_____

_____

_____

_____

_____

_____

_____

_____

_____

_____

_____

_____

_____

What "random" things seem to be happening right now? How might these situations actually be God's guiding hand, preparing you for a new chapter in your life?

_____

_____

_____

_____

_____

_____

_____

_____

_____

_____

_____

_____

Set Right

God was pleased to have all his fullness dwell in him, and through him to reconcile to himself all things, whether things on earth or things in heaven, by making peace through his blood, shed on the cross. Once you were alienated from God and were enemies in your minds because of your evil behavior. But now he has reconciled you by Christ's physical body through death to present you holy in his sight, without blemish and free from accusation.

COLOSSIANS 1:19–22

SET RIGHT

I knew what I had to do. I just hoped for another way out. I had broken my nose in a basketball game and had two raccoon eyes. I needed to have my nose reset, but I knew that only meant more pain. I met a surgeon at the hospital and, after giving me the once-over, he told me he could reset my nose with no problem. I had two choices: go under anesthesia, which he called the sissy expensive way, or I could just let him reset my tender and wounded nose right then and there.

I chose the sissy way. I knew what I should have done, but I wanted the easier way out. The doctor said he needed to "survey the land" once again. He placed his hand over my nose with a pretty tight grip and said, "This is where it hurts, right?" And just when I thought, "Surely he won't," surely he did. He grabbed my two displaced nose bones and jerked them back into their proper God-given position.

After they peeled me off the ceiling, I was OK. And though mildly shocked, I was greatly relieved that my nose was set right. Even though my little episode was no major trauma, it is a good example of how we often hope for the least painful way out.

There was one occasion when all of Jesus' disciples suffered something much worse than my broken nose. Jesus told them their close friend Lazarus was asleep. Jesus said they were going into Judea where Lazarus lived. Now they all knew Jesus wasn't very popular in Judea. In fact, the authorities wanted to kill him. So they quite naturally chose the least painful way to deal with the situation. They said to Jesus, "If Lazarus is asleep, don't you think he'll wake up?"

Then Jesus gave them the bad news. Lazarus was dead. And they were going into Judea. Why? Because Jesus had a plan. He wanted to bring Lazarus back from the dead so his disciples would understand who he was—the Son of God in the flesh. Yes, it would be a difficult time. But once they saw Lazarus walk out of that open tomb, they knew things had been set right, and the tough times were worth it.

When I broke my nose, I didn't want the doctor to set it right then and there. I wanted the easy way. When Lazarus became ill and Jesus wanted his disciples to go with him into the hostile territory of Judea, they didn't want to go. They wanted Jesus to heal him from a distance. But that was nothing compared to what came next.

Jesus went into Judea again. And this time he was captured, put through a mock trial, and crucified on a Roman cross. And for his disciples, there was no easy way out. The one who turned Jesus in to the authorities killed himself. Another refused to admit he'd ever known Jesus. They were all terrified. But then Jesus was raised from the dead. And 11 of Jesus' 12 disciples learned an important lesson. The easy way isn't always the best way. When they saw their resurrected Lord, they knew everything, for all eternity, had been set right.

—Greg Allen

169

In what situations have you tried to take the least painful route out? Was that the best way?

_____

_____

_____

_____

_____

_____

_____

_____

_____

_____

_____

_____

When have you chosen to take the painful, but right, way out?
What was the outcome?

_____

_____

_____

_____

_____

_____

171

_____

_____

_____

_____

_____

_____

_____

Your Biggest Fan

Fear not, for I have redeemed you;

> *I have summoned you by name; you are mine. . . .*

You are precious and honored in my sight,

> *And . . . I love you.*

ISAIAH 43:1, 4

YOUR BIGGEST FAN

Mozart would discover his other-worldly talent under the careful instruction of his father, a gifted musician. Beethoven developed under the finest of teachers, allowing his remarkable gift to blossom and grow to maturity. But Gustav Mahler, one of the greatest conductors to ever hold a baton, would discover and demonstrate his gift in his grandpa's attic. The love that only a grandfather can have for one of his grandchildren would give 5-year-old Mahler his first taste of the empowering and remarkable sensation of someone believing in him.

As a young boy Gustav Mahler did not know the joys of a happy home. His parents barely tolerated each other, and as the oldest surviving child, he would witness the death of five of his siblings. His father ran a small distillery that put food on the table, but that was about it. And father would expect son to take over the family business.

It would be a visit to his grandparents' home that would go a long way toward setting the course of his life. He and his brothers and sisters were allowed to play up in the attic, and while they were exploring, Gustav had his first encounter with a piano, such as it was. Old and quite battered, the tinny, out-of-tune hulk excited the young boy's curiosity. The instrument was so large and the child so small that he had to stand on his tiptoes to reach the keys, which he couldn't even see. With his hands held high he began to play all sorts of tunes he'd heard before. He managed to play them so recognizably that his parents and grandparents came upstairs to discover where the music was coming from. When they saw the little guy reaching up to play the keys, they were astonished.

The wheels were turning in Grandpa's head. He asked little Gustav if he would like to have a toy like that at home, and you can imagine the excited, gleeful response. With what Mahler calls "indescribable delight" the very next day he was surprised by the arrival of the monstrous piano at his front door after its having been trundled to his house on an oxcart. It was a grandfather's faith in his grandson that would convince Mahler's father to acknowledge and support his son's musical gift. And the seeds of musical greatness were planted in the life of this little boy all because his grandfather believed in him.

Life is greatly enriched when people believe in us and utterly impoverished when we do not experience some measure of confidence from another. It wouldn't be the same if my wife didn't believe in me. In fact, she considers me capable of a great deal more than I think I can do. I could not be a minister if the people I lead and teach did not believe in me.

But circumstances can change. People can die. Life can take just about everything away in an instant. What then? When I'm alone who will say, "You can do it, you've got what it takes, I believe in you"? Maybe that's where you think you are right now, alone with your self-doubt and misgivings. But you're not.

The Bible tells us there is one who considers your life so valuable and believes in you so completely that he gave his life so that you might live—so confident is he of what you have to offer. He is described as one who sticks closer than a brother. The apostle Paul even went so far as to say, "I can do everything through Christ who gives me strength." Paul certainly wasn't boasting. He knew what you can know too—the Lord is your biggest fan!

—Dan Stuecher

Who has believed in you and helped you realize your potential?
What things did they do to encourage you?

_____

_____

_____

_____

_____

_____

_____

_____

_____

_____

_____

_____

_____

How has God shown you that you are special to him? How has he encouraged you?

_____

_____

_____

_____

_____

_____

_____

_____

_____

_____

_____

_____

Keep Going

He who began a good work in you will carry it on to completion

until the day of Christ Jesus.

PHILIPPIans 1:6

KEEP GOING

In the first years of the 20th century, Cincinnati was one of the 10 largest cities in the country. The city planners decided to drain the Miami-Erie canal running through the western side of town and build a subway in its place. The public and local politicians supported the idea, and they voted to spend six million dollars to build the tunnels.

But then came World War I and with it a lack of supplies and manpower. By the end of the war, the cost of steel and concrete had doubled. By 1925, the money had run out with only 11 of the 16 tunnels completed. Then the Depression and World War II depleted what was left of popular support for the project, and what had been started was left incomplete.

Those same subway tunnels remain in reasonably good condition to this very day, in spite of the fact they were never completed. In 1957 the city installed a water main through two miles of the tunnels. In the '60s, city planners installed water containers and radio gear to use the tunnels as a nuclear fallout shelter, if necessary. I was actually in those tunnels once and it's a pretty amazing place.

But those subway tunnels have never been used for their original purpose, and the failure to complete the project delayed Cincinnati's development at a crucial time in its history. It's not always easy to finish what we start. Do you ever wonder how God finishes everything he starts? Or how he has the patience to continue when the going gets tough?

Paderewski was a famous Polish composer. As he was in the wings preparing to present a piano concert to a large crowd, he watched a child in the audience slip away from his mother and head straight for the huge Steinway piano on stage. Within seconds the little boy was playing "Chopsticks."

The crowd began to shout, "Get that kid out of here! He'll ruin the piano." Paderewski grabbed his jacket and rushed onto the stage. Ignoring the shouting of the crowd, he reached behind the boy and began playing the countermelody to "Chopsticks." As they played, Paderewski began to whisper in the boy's ear, "Keep going. Don't quit."

Sometimes it feels like we have nothing to offer—that everyone is yelling at us to get off the stage. But the master knows our value and sees our potential. And unlike the tunnel builders in Cincinnati, he finishes what he starts. God the Father, the maestro of life, delights in encouraging us to keep going. And with him playing the countermelody, our song is beautiful.

—Jennifer Taylor for Rick Rusaw

In what ways do you feel that you're being told to "get off the stage"? What are you trying to finish?

_____

_____

_____

_____

_____

_____

_____

_____

_____

_____

_____

_____

How does knowing that God is still working *on* you and *with* you change your outlook on those things you are struggling to complete?

_____

_____

_____

_____

_____

_____

_____

_____

_____

_____

_____

_____

_____

■■ WINDOWS OF WORSHIP™

Devotions in this book are based on scripts first delivered by Paul Williams and the following hosts for *Worship*.

GREG ALLEN is a worship minister at Southeast Christian Church in Louisville, Kentucky, where he has served since 1983.

RICK RUSAW is senior minister at LifeBridge Christian Church in Longmont, Colorado, where he has served since 1991.

DAN STUECHER is senior minister at Harborside Christian Church in Safety Harbor, Florida, a congregation he founded in 1984.

Be sure to read and give these other Windows of Worship™ devotional journals.

ISBN 0-7847-1514-9
25001

ISBN 0-7847-1516-5
25003